Whatever Happened to Baby Wayne?

Wayne F. Burke

Hog Press

Hog Press
an imprint of Culicidae Press®
PO Box 5069
Madison, WI 53705-5069
hogpress.com
editor@hogpress.com

Hog Press

WHATEVER HAPPENED TO BABY WAYNE?
Copyright © 2025 by Wayne F. Burke
All rights reserved.

No part of this book may be reproduced in any form by any electronic or mechanized means (including photocopying, recording, or information storage and retrieval) without written permission, except in the case of brief quotations embodied in critical articles and reviews. For more information, please visit culicidaepress.com

ISBN: 978-1-68315-133-3

Our books may be purchased in bulk for promotional, educational or business use. Please contact your local bookseller or the Culicidae Press Sales Department at +1-352-215-7558 or by email at sales@culicidaepress.com

culicidaepress.bsky.social – facebook.com/culicidaepress
threads.net/@culicidaepress – instagram.com/culicidaepress
x.com/culicidaepress

Design by polytekton © 2025
Cover image of entry to the Basilica di Santa Maria in Aracoeli in Rome, Italy, by polytekton @2016

Dedication

Dedicated to all the readers who have read my books; who have bought one or more of my books; who have told another person about one of my books, or more than one of my books; who have written blurbs for any of my books; and who have given me a 'Like' on FB or on Good Reads, or a review, or a comment, publicly or privately, for anything of mine they have read there or elsewhere. Readers! Without you all would be lost.

Table of Contents

Dedication	3
SECTION I	
ALL FOR GLORY	8
Ache	10
J C PENNY	12
Wail	14
Holy Moly	16
Glory	19
The All-Star	20
Coach	21
History	22
Old	25
Candy	26
Credit	28
Day Dreaming	29
News	30
Croutonville	32
Asshole	33
A Pro	34
A New Friend	35
Soup	36

Sunday Morning	39
Half-Acre	40
Chill	41
My Uncle	42
Barre, VT	45
Writing	46
Class	47
Slip	48
Good Cop	49
Sticks	50
Coffee	51
Al	52
Ale	53
Innocent	56
Speed Racer	58
Piss Test	62

Section II
OUT OF MY MIND   64

Dream   65
Purgatory   66
Rommel Swallows Cyanide   67
October 21ˢᵗ   68
Vein   69
Secrets   70
Abe   71
Dead   72
Bill   73
Cosmology   74
Lassitude Sets In And   75
Ate Oatmeal this Morning   76
Igloos   77
Told myself   79
Sunset   84
Friends   85
Catholic   86
Play   87
Gabble Goop   88
Advise   89
Honey,   90
Death   91
Vacay   93
Sinners   94
Storm   97
Friend   99
Cold Snow World   100
A Nice Winter Day of   101
Dream   102
The Scary War   103
Nietzsche   105

Not Forgive	106
Under the Volcano	107
Big Man	108
Stiff	111
I Am	112
Dying	113
Hidden	114
Attack	117
Out Back	118
No Poetry	119
Paul Bearer	120
Acknowledgements	123

SECTION I

ALL FOR GLORY

1.

they died without a peep; died
with drawers full
of paid receipts and
ledgers, ink-stained
with thumb prints,
that recorded only the
story of dollars
earned and spent:
the gas station and
the INN—
the car that went from home
to work and back; the
early mornings and late
nights in the cold & dark,
the rolls of nickels
stored in a metal box
along with insurance policies
that never paid enough
to make a difference
in anyone's life.

Ache

I left the ballgame with
stomach ache, and
walked off the field
with Gramp, his
hand on my shoulder:
"You must have patience,
my boy," he said.
I did not need advice—
Grandma gave more than
enough—
I did need the hand on
my shoulder though (something
Grandma never gave).
My stomach ached for days.
Gramp drove me to the hospital
in the big city.
I lay on the examination table
on top the crinkly paper—
a young man doctor told me
to roll over.
After he pulled my pants down
I pulled them back up.
"I have to look," he said,
his face red.
"Let him," Gramp said,
his face also red…
On the ride home
Gramp told me that
I had worms.
The windshield wipers beat in time
so what
so what

"how did I get worms?"
"From something you ate."
I thought of things I had eaten
as rain smeared the windshield
and the wipers picked up the tempo:
tough luck
tough luck
tough luck.

J C PENNY

"Keep your hands to yourselves,"
Grandma crabs as
we walk down the carpeted aisle.
"Do not touch anything!"

My brother has to touch something
and is slapped
and bawls
and is told to sit
while Grandma picks out clothes
for us to try on, first scrutinizing each price tag,
her mouth downturned, like a horseshoe,
in a frown.

We walk before her in revue…
She cannot decide, and
starts to pick at a wart
on her cheek—
pulls a Kleenex from her purse
dabs her
eyes then cleans her
glasses.

I tell her what to buy
but she does not listen, and
turns, instead, to the clerk, a guy
who smirks, in response.

I wander through the
clothes racks
and am called back
and told
"stay put."

My brother sucks his thumb.

Grandma, before the cash
register, says to the cashier:
"They do not give them away
do they?"

We are carried out with the packages
to the car
a chariot
that returns us home
"at last!" Grandma says.

Wail

I sang a song about my
Uncle
while the birds
chirped, and I went up & down
in the backyard swing.

It was summer.

My brother jumped off the
other swing and
ran inside the house.

The blue sky swung with me:
The back door of the house
opened and shut with a bang, and
my uncle
ran down the porch steps—

a svelte two hundred eighty
pounds and five foot five;
he had his belt off
before crossing the
driveway, the belt dangling from
his hand like a black snake.

I ran, but
at his command
stopped.

He held me by the wrist as
he beat me with the belt
and I squirmed like a worm
on a hook.

Mr. Larson, next door, on his carport
ducked a little lower behind his
lawn mower.
Old man Decensi
across the street,
sat on his screened-in porch
looking like a shadow.

Holy Moly

"Some Catholics you kids are!"
Grandma scolds as
she ushers us out the
door, Palm Sunday—
"hurry! You are going to be
late!"
We walk without haste to the
car.
My sister drives. My brother, in the
front seat, gives
driving instructions.
A mile down the road
Sister snaps "SHUT UP!
GO TO HELL!"
My brother says
he will tell Grandma of the
language Sister uses, and
a seething silence ensues.
The smoke stack of the
textile factory is higher
than the church steeple.
Sister does not dip her fingers
into the holy water fount as
we enter;
just before mass begins
she walks out;
her soul, I know
is black as coal:
mine is white with a touch
of venial gray—
during the sermon
my brother falls asleep, cheek

on the varnished pew,
a string of drool from his mouth—
I punch him and
he wakes, but
instead of thanking me, for
saving his immortal soul,
he whips me
on the ride home
with a palm
taken from the church.

2.

April and start of
Spring training—
reading biography of Ty Cobb

before the ballgame
the groundskeepers
are the game

Glory

It was all for the glory—
chasing down the ball-carrier
slamming my helmeted-head into
a gut, running over the
catcher, because Coach told me to:
I never knew
then
the glory was his, not mine, though
won with my blood,
my guts, and
all for nothing but
to make him look good, and
for some shits' profits,
and for the prestige of the
school, that
spit some of us out each year
into the factories and
fields, where our fathers, uncles, and
brothers—who had also worn the
red & white uniform, labored
for what they too
never knew.

The All-Star

He had the good wheels and
the good arm, good stick too
(but never did hit in the
clutch) and after being drafted
by a Major League team, he
went to camp, but got cut
and quit
cold turkey;
he did not have the guts
to stick it out, continue;
he flushed his dream
down the toilet
and returned to the
old home town and
a cushy job with
probation & parole
and a seat on a stool
at CHICK'S LOUNGE where
he was pointed to, as
The Kid Who Almost Made It.

Coach

Church League basketball practice,
Tuesday night
at the armory,
green & white the colors
of Saint Thomas Aquinas:
the coach, my uncle
stood beneath the basket,
passed the ball to us
as we ran in for lay-ups'
my turn came
and he whipped the ball,
it smashed me in the face;
his laughed his laugh, cheeks
like plums
in his fat face;
some of the players laughed too
but uneasily, and
in the locker room
Dicky, a forward, asked me
"how can you take that from him?"
And I had nothing to say,
no answer,
did not even know
then
that I had a choice.

History

If I had done what
I was going to do long ago
becoming a High School teacher and
coach, I would be long dead, I am
sure: penned in the little town of my birth
with people without imagination enough to dream
and me married, to my High School sweetheart, a nun
in the making, and with kids
a house,
a dog,
a mortgage,
forget it—
I would be early in the cemetery, my tombstone
above ground, flowers on my grave on
anniversary days, and
my footprints all over the
mountains, from me trying to get the hell out
but unable.

3.

solo flight to the
Planet Crouton,
helmet on

Old

A logjam at the EXIT
of the supermarket:
an elderly couple doddering
in the doorway…
A woman with cart load ahead of
me: "What are they doing?" she
demands. "Plow into them," I say.
"No, I won't."
A woman behind says: "They do not
give a shit about anybody."
The white-haired codger
tugs on his missus' sleeve as
they move, slow as cold
molasses…
The woman ahead gives me
a 'look', eyes above her
black mask.
I feel like kicking her
in the ass. "They are old," I say, but
neither woman, front or back
gives a shit
about that.

Candy

A fat girl standing in the
doorway of WALGREENS
"can you buy me something?
I have not eaten all day."
She follows me inside.
Tells me her name, "Jen."
"What's yours?"
"Wayne."
"Duane?"
"Yeah. Duane."
In the candy aisle she plucks a bag of
Peanut Butter M & Ms off a shelf, on
sale 2 for 8 dollars.
"Can I have two?"
"Sure."
She scoots down the center aisle
and around a corner:
returns with a pint of ice cream.
On the way to check-out, I notice
she has three bags of candy and
I tell her put one back.
At check-out she has something
to say to everyone.
Asks a woman why she, the
woman, is buying so many
diapers. Compliments another
on her attire. At the register
she introduces me to the
cashier: "This is Duane, he is
helping me. I have not eaten
all day." The cashier has polished
nails; she and Jen

have a lot to say to one another
about fingernails. Finally,
I get to pay. Outside the store
she calls "thank you!" and
I grunt "okay," not
begrudging her the food
but hoping she does not make
a habit of asking.

Credit

I go up to the store counter to pay
for my sandwich
and discover that
I do not have my wallet on me.
"That's alright," the counter-guy says, "pay
me the next time."
I thank him and leave, feeling
a little ashamed because
I have never liked the guy—
have disparaged him in my head
repeatedly—
it is the first time
anyone in this town
has extended credit to
me…
Not so bad a burgh, this town
after all
I tell myself, tootling down the
sun-lit sidewalk. Not so ugly a dump,
suddenly: not as hostile seeming…
"Don't go back there," a voice
in my head says.
"Fuck 'em."

Day Dreaming

while walking down the street
I step off a curb and
a car flashes past...
the width of a coat of paint
between us: "whoa!"
one of the yahoos inside
yells, as
the car swerves
and I catch my breath, check
to see if my leg
still attached, then
get pissed, and
scream
"You ASSHOLE!"
But the car,
already to the
end of the street,
does not even
hear me.

News

He walks up to me
on the sidewalk: a little guy,
egg-shaped head,
glasses: "They stole my
car," he says.
"No shit."
"Yeah. I had it parked in the
library parking lot."
"How did they do it?"
"I don't know. Still have my key."
He shows me the key.
"The cops gave me a ride home."
"That is too bad."
"Yeah."
"Well, good luck to you."
"Thanks."
I walk away, wondering if
I could have done more for the
guy: drove him around to look for the car?
A week later: same guy, same
sidewalk: "hey, they stole my car."
"Is that right?"
"Yeah. I had it parked in the
supermarket parking lot."
"You get a lot of cars stolen from you
don't you?"
"The cops are looking for it."
"Oh. Well, maybe they will find it."
"Yeah."
"Well, good luck," I say.

He calls to me as I walk away:
"Afghanistan has fallen!"
"Oh geeze," I say.
"Oh GEEZE."

Croutonville

Leaves skitter along the
pavement, sun peeks from
behind a cloud on
a quiet afternoon, nothing
out of line in the city—
a couple walk along the street,
arguing; the man begins to
shout; the woman reverses
direction; the man chases her;
she swings her pocketbook at him
like a bat; he picks up something
fallen from the pocketbook and
throws it at her...
"You hit me!" she cries. "YOU HIT ME!"
"Why do you act like this?" he shouts.
"It is over! OVER!" she screams. "Help!
Someone call the cops!"
Leaves rush past my feet, an army of
them, running for
their lives...
A cop car shows up.
Then another.
The couple has already moved on, their
voices distant: meanwhile, leaves
scabber along the sidewalks of
Croutonville.

Asshole

I am standing in line
at WALGREENS
when a guy, walking
by me, and toward the
exit, points and
says "that register is open."
He wears a baseball cap and
has a front tooth missing.
"Did you hear me? Down there—
it is open."
"Take a hike."
"Excuse me!? What did you say?"
"You heard me."
"You do not need to be rude.
I am only telling you…I work here."
"Take a long hike."
He stalks off, muttering.
I move to the register:
The clerk tells me that
the guy does work in the place.
"I did not know that."
She rings up my purchase
without another word said
and I slink out of there, knowing
I have been an asshole
and should apologize, but
the guy is long gone
unless
waiting for me
around the corner.

A Pro

I am sitting on a park bench
and eating lunch, when
I see her approaching:
a big girl with long auburn hair
and front teeth like CHICKLETS:
"Excuse me! Sir! Would you
have some spare change? Or
maybe a few dollars?"
Her car, she says, needs gasoline.
The ATM machine at her bank
will not, for some reason, dispense
cash, and Door Dash has
hindered her, in some way that
she fails to specify, or
maybe she does, but
I've stopped listening, as
I drag my wallet
out, extract a few bills--
and suddenly recall her
standing outside the Chinese Restaurant
one brutally cold winter day,
no gloves on her hands, no hat on
her head; she jerked a couple tears out
then (easier to do in the cold) before
I got the wallet out of my pocket…

A pro.

A New Friend

She stood in the
shadow of the parking lot, waved
and said hello as I walked past
I said how are you?
She said are you looking for love?
Said she gave love to people
nice to her.
I said and how much do these people
pay for love?
$100 she said.
And where do you go with these people?
To her room, or
anywhere else they want to go.
I said not in the mood
just now
she gave me her phone number
and a hug
said my face was handsome
I asked if she was broke
she said yes
I gave her $20
she said call me
I said
I have your number.

Soup

"Holy shit," I remark, "a lot of
money for soup." The
glasses-wearing shaven-head
guy behind the
cash register asks "you want
your money back?" "No,
I am just saying—seems a lot."
The counter-woman arrives
with my soup. "Here—take
your money back," the guy
says. "I will take the soup,"
I say. The guy throws my dollar bills
down on the counter,
barks "NO YOU WON'T!"
I wad the bills together and
throw them at his face.
He stalks around the counter:
"GET OUT!"
Stands toe to toe—his egg-head
above my nose. "Get out! You
old bastard!"
"Old? Eat shit!"
We exchange insults concerning
each other's mother.
He follows me to the door:
"Get off my back!" I bark.
He gives me a shove and
I hit the sidewalk, get up, run
to the door, scream, "OUTSIDE!"

It has been a long time since
I have felt rage. A voice that
is not mine escapes my throat:
"GET THE FUCK OUT HERE!"
The guy comes to the door, says
cops are on the way. So
what? He retreats inside--
lucky for him, and
for me too, I guess--because I would
have beat the prick or else
been beaten--did not matter which,
to me.

4.

born in Youngstown
died in Tombstone

Sunday Morning

Church bells ringing
and a priest, on
television, makes the sign
of the cross—
Grandma says her rosary
Grampa returns with the
Sunday newspaper;
my brother and sister fight
over the Comics section;
my uncle rises from bed
in time to watch 'Community Auditions'—
steam from the kitchen,
kettle on the stove whistles,
smell of pot roast in the
holy air.

Half-Acre

Mowing the lawn one of my
"jobs" though I never asked
for or agreed to—
my uncle said I would be
paid to do it, 50-cents
but I never did see any
money: my uncle jiggled
the coins inside his jug-head,
told me be satisfied with
what I had, room & board
(lucky to get that!).
He let me live in his house,
that was enough, he said.
He was a kind bastard and
generous shit.
I polished his shoes and
ran his errands but
that never stopped him from
giving me back-handed slaps
or kicks from size-10 shoes…
I used to aim the shotgun
at him, and
fire a blast or two, but
no bolt or bullets in the gun,
it could hurt no one, it
stood useless, in the closet
with the clothes.

Chill

Drops dripping from icicles
on a rare day of sunshine
in cold inhospitable
February
formidable as
my grandmother
in her chair
a bottle at her feet
cigarette in her hand
smoke curling above
a beehive hairdo like a haystack
her goggle-eyes of
reproach and
icy smile
stopped me cold
on approach…
The drops sparkle
like the lenses of her glasses
whenever the sun
broke through the gloom
of that second-floor apartment
room
where love was frozen
solid.

My Uncle

the fat man—who
ran the gas station
my father once ran—
barked orders
around the
house—using the
back of his hand
and his belt
to enforce
his commands.
His shouts filled the rooms
as his body bulked
the floors that creaked
and sagged beneath
his leather shoes that
squeaked like mice.

5.

poetry does not get you to the
Hall of Fame
only
through the
night

Barre, VT

I sit at a table
in the sun
outside of a restaurant
on the Champs Elysees—
a hell of a Paris
this town is—
sketchy characters, assorted
specimens
walk past
and the gyro or giro or
gismo sandwich
I have ordered,
is not hot,
and cost me twelve dollars—
qu'es que c'est
with that?

Writing

This writing I do
may add up to
something: some
kind of living is
my hope, which
is a joke. Maybe
a grant, but who
will grant it? Maybe
a position, top or
bottom (I will take
either). Most of my
words will go, I fear
with me onto the
funeral pyre.

Class

My old girlfriend said
that I would be a classy guy
if I dressed better and
stopped picking my nose,
but the price, to me
seemed high;
my jacket was torn at the elbows,
I had holes in my socks,
and the nose thing
it was habit
from when
as a kid
I was bored--
I was anxious...
I did not really care
anyway
about being "classy."

Slip

A strong wind sweeps up a girl's
skirt;
she has a slip-on underneath,
and underneath that,
nothing.
After she goes into the café
I wait, outside
for her return
but,
by the time she does
return,
the damn wind has died
down.

Good Cop

The cop told me
I would have to stay
in jail
over the weekend
if I could not pay the
ten-dollar bail.
I called my brother
who lived on the other side of the
state, but
he was not at home
or else not picking up his telephone—
it looked like I was stuck
on the metal slab
behind steel bars, but
a different cop, an older guy—
could have been my uncle—
volunteered
out of nowhere
to lend me the money, and
him—though I was not then
paying bills of any kind—
him I paid back.

Sticks

October afternoon and
some clown juggling
sticks, in the park—
an escapee from the circus
who slept with the
Tattooed Lady
who was married to the
Strong Man
who threatened the clown—
a sad melodrama
the clown ran from
his big gun-boat shoes flopping
and bright red nose
scaring the children
all along the road
to the next town.

Coffee

Met an old crony of mine
on the street
he asked
how you been?
What do you say?
Before I could answer
he gave me his views
on national, international, and
local news, then asked
if I had a couple bucks to spare,
enough for a coffee, and
I said "sure," and he took the
bills and said "see you later"
and I watched him go, remembering
when I used to drink those 'coffees'
too.

Al

Albert put a bullet into the
steeple of Saint Stan's church
at 3 a.m.
using his brother's 30-aught-6 rifle
and shooting from
his bedroom window;
his mother came running, fearing
the worst;
the cops came with guns drawn—
Albert said he did not want to go
with the cops;
his mother said he was a "good boy," but
would not take his medicine.
Albert fought the cops all the way to the
car, then
called them "pigs" from the back seat
while they drove him to the
nut house.

Ale

Pale green ocean the
color of bottled Ballentine Ale—
a six pack on the
windowsill
and seagulls on the
gravel roof below; dirty city birds
like wise-guys, beady-eyed, and
with hooked beaks
like war clubs of the Iroquois—
after drinking 5 of the bottles
and trying, unsuccessfully
to piss on the birds, and
having solved, in my mind
half the world's problems,
I drink the last, then
decide, the other half
not worth thinking about, and
go out
into the city, with
trouble
following so close
behind, it
steps on my heels
whenever I halt.

6.

Need a Dear-y
to be less
dreary. But no
gott meine
Herren. Nein
gots. Vhere
gets? Choich
for virgin Mary?

I mention her mood swings:
there are things about my
personality, she says

rain drops like laser
beams shatter to
crystal shards

Innocent

I was in grade school, but
used to hang around with older guys
of the neighborhood.

Chief Larson, in sixth grade
(I was third) asked me if I knew
how babies were made.

It was a summer afternoon.
We stood in the Garibaldi's driveway:
Jackie Garibaldi swung a baseball bat;
Davy Baguette threw a jack-knife,
sticking it into the lawn.

"From prolonged kissing," I said.

Chief, Davy, and Jackie hee-hawed like
jackasses.

"It was your mother and father," Chief hollered.
"You fuckin' nut!"
He made a circular-shaped hole using his index finger and
thumb, and ran his other index finger in and out
the hole.
"Like that!"

I ran, across the lawn and
across the road and into
my yard.
Laughter from across the street
hurt my ears.

Maybe their parents had done "it"
like Chief said—
and thinking of their parents, I could
believe it, but
my parents
would never have done
any such thing.

Speed Racer

Outside, the snow falls
thick as fleece
and
I am kneeling in the
snow, again.

On top of the hill at the
top of our street.
With Jigs Garibaldi, red flushed face, ice
balls like ornaments
off a Christmas tree hanging from
his toque.

We watch the approach, up hill
of flat-footed Denny Larson
a flabby mama's boy,
pulling a sled behind him.

"You are not using that, are you?"
Jigs says in disbelief.

"Yes I am using it," Denny crabs.

Snowflakes the size of leaves
fall from the gray sky.

Denny lies belly-down.

"Wait!" Jigs says, looking to the
right and down slope.
"Where is Sondrini?"

Sondrini, our look-out
is nowhere in sight.

Denny shoves himself to the
lip of the hill.
"Get out of the way!" he hollers.

The sled starts down, just as
a car comes into view, moving
along the snow-covered road.

"WAIT!!!!"

The sled moves like a bullet downhill.

Denny and sled disappear beneath the
car.
The car's right rear goes up
then down.
Denny lies on the roadside
atop his sled…

"Speak to us, Denny!" Weed Garibaldi begs.

Eyes closed, face white; a line of
dark blood from corner of his mouth
to his chin.

Spike, Skully, and Weed stand
gawking.

"I never even seen him," the teenage driver
says, his jacket red & white
with the school's colors.

"Call an ambulance!" Jigs screams.

A door in the Carnazola's block opens
and shuts with a bang
and refrigerator-sized Mrs. Carnazola, wearing a housedress and
flip-flops, throws
her hands up:
"Oh my god! His poor mother!"

A cop car ambles, down the
road, moving slow as molasses.
The car's red lights cut through
the gathering darkness.

An ambulance sounds, far off
in the distance.

"Give him room!" the cop says.

I walk off, down our street
through the thickening snow
falling thick as fleece.

Mrs. Larson suddenly emerges,
a shawl over her shoulders
kerchief on head.
I do not know what to say or do.

She skates past me, unbuckled galoshes
on her feet
shuffling.

Piss Test

The nurse, wearing a starched white
uniform, says
"come with me," and
I follow her
down a long corridor to
a small bathroom.

"Stand there," she says, pointing
to a spot by the door.

I stand still—to show her
how good and obedient
I am.

She turns from a cabinet and
places a small plastic cup
on top of the tank of the toilet
in the corner.

"You see that cup?
I want you to make number one
in it. Do you understand?"
I nod
and she leaves the room.

I look at the cup:
so far away.
Why? How do I—
It is a test, I think.
To see how far, how accurate—
I take my bibet out and aim:
pee splatters on the face of the
toilet. I zero-in and loop some of the
golden stream into the cup.

I zip up, proud of myself.
I wonder if other kids have done as well
on the test.

A rap on the door and
the nurse enters.
She stares at the toilet:
"What have you done?" she screeches.

She stars pulling paper towels from the
dispenser as if
yanking the hair
from
my head.

Section II

OUT OF MY MIND

1.

Dream

awarded a gold pen
by "Writers of America"—
the pen
also detects levels of
carbon monoxide

Purgatory

Thou shalt not steal
or feel
or deal from the bottom
of the deck (no matter
how stacked against you)
so help you
god almighty will strike you
dead, deader
than a doornail
or email never sent,
you will go to Purgatory
and sit, waiting, 20,000 years
with hands in your lap, speaking
only when spoken to, the
magazines on the rack
dog-eared, thumbed through:
LIFE, LOOK, HIGHLIGHTS
(find the hidden items in the
picture: cat, dog, key, louse,
yourself...) the nurse
will call when God is ready.

Rommel Swallows Cyanide

No one comes to visit
me: wonder how long
I would lie, dead
inside this a.p.t.?
The landlord would miss
his rent in a month;
mail would slowly build
in the box;
people at work might
call the cops:
Richard Brautigan, who was getting
50-grand
a book
while he was hot,
lay for a headless month
on the 2nd floor
of his house
while flies and
maggots visited.

October 21st

The day of Kerouac's death;
he went and
planted himself in the
railroad earth: should
have stuck to AA, Jack
and become grand old
man of letters; of course
had you 'stuck' you
would have had to become
some other
maybe a Norman Podhoretz
type, or
Robert Giroux (remember how they
shit on you? Of course you do.)
I guess you were fated to
leave this mortal-ed coil
at age 47: to croak in
unchangeableness and
become legend.

Vein

Cannot drink anymore coffee
because I am
coffee-ed out, like
Balzac
in his shack
good-to-the-last-drop
java
in my veins
even the one they took
out of my leg and
sewed onto my
heart, that
flaccid bag
occupying space in the
chambers of my
conception,
and me
still conceiving,
and almost as
well as I ever have.

Secrets

of mumbled childhood
hidden in locked drawers and
pocketbooks with clasps—
in scrapbooks with iron
covers; in washrooms of
cellars and underground with
skeletons in boxes, and
behind altars where
god lived in shadows, like
on a dark country road
without houses, just
trees that said
"schussh!"
whenever the wind
blew.

Abe

A new book out
on Lincoln
I read—
I've read a lot
of them, books
on Lincoln:
not a city lot
or a car lot
but a load of
books
on Lincoln,
that son of a gun,
that turkey;
his wife was kind of a witch
his son became kind of rich
and he managed
his war better
than Johnson
done.

Dead

August lingers like
an uninvited party
guest;
everyone is on vacation
or else they've died and
turned gray as the
statues in the park—
dead as the old days,
as the old ways—
dead as the brain cells
of those who do not
use them; dead
like the moon, like
Latin, like this town,
like my aunt's stillborn
baby: lifeless, nameless,
almost forgotten.

Bill

the table slides into
place—
the booth is a capsule
I am riding into
space
with the New York Times beside
me;
the waitress,
a distant galaxy
hovering
in space/time
arrival with the
check: $5.56,
as Lincoln,
grim as a sailor
in a squall,
takes the scene in
with his green eyes.

Cosmology

The sky is a river
flowing through the
clouds, which
are rocks
banked along the
river's edge,
but the rocks are
moving too
like everything else
one big free-for-all
that the earth
is passing through—
the whole thing
balanced on
the shoulders
of someone
with a name
you do not hear
anymore,
like "Valmore"
or "Silvester."

Lassitude Sets In And

the chair begins to sit
on me;
a fan turns its idiot head
blowing a breeze, and
I solidify, like quartz
and
nod out
nada
as traffic sweeps the
highway and
suchness spreads at
finite limits of
infinite space, like
the Blob of
silent flow, viscous
and deadly, and
coming to
a theater near you
soon.

Ate Oatmeal this Morning

to get off the eggs.
From the egg
it all began
but had to be some
hen
some henry miller
type
the cosmodemonic
omelet
with everything on it
the kitchen sink
pots
pans
a tar paper roll
a Great Dane,
you name it,
one big
soufflé.

Igloos

June and cold here
and wet: it is not
fair—the short summer
should blaze like a gasoline
fire, with red sky and
sultry nights, air like
velvet on my skin; but
this is the North, land of
ice and cold wind, land
where the Igloo people
live—those who turn
lobster-red in the
sun and wear
long-sleeved shirts plus
boots
all year round…
Fur on their faces.

golden cloud heads
like busts of
clouds
achieved greatness
in their time

from green to orange
the leaves
my life
changing tone
too

Told myself

"self
do not draw in 3-dollar notebooks
no more, draw
in a sketch pad
(though you have to lug one
around) you
ding-dong,
and not in a pocket book either
unless, of course
you want to carry one,
honey."

One number off
the lottery, the
story of my life
lately, an inch
shy, a dollar
short; because
how the planets line up
maybe,
or the way the goddamn
cookie crumbles,
or is it god, terrible
Yahweh, who
killed Job's children
in order to teach him a lesson?
(But tell me—
what lesson did the
children learn?)

Black tar parking lot
bisected by white
lines, stained with
artwork by Tapies
black on black,
oil splotches,
skid marks—
Franz Kline…
Shadows of buildings
cut squares
blacker than
asphalt.

Van Gogh the insufferable 'fixer',
who knew best, and was not slow
to let others know it: gave pointers
to his sister-in-law on how to raise
her son. Sent a steady diet of
suggestions to Theo on how to live
("do just what I've advised you"), ditto,
his sister Will. Like the lives of all the
'fixers', Van Gogh's life best described as
a 'mess'. The times people did allow
him to 'fix' them—like the prostitute Sien,
whom Vincent tried to reform—he was
happiest. But when others rebelled (Gauguin)
or failed to take his advice, he became an
unhappy camper.

Got a booth
to myself
in the restaurant;
only the waitress
and, later, the
cashier to interact
with (unless the waitress
takes the check up);
I can talk to the other
seat if I want to:
"Hi, how are you?
"You look lovely in green leather."
I can write an Op-Ed piece
for the newspaper (fuck that)
or I can pour ketchup on
myself and pretend I was
wounded in Vietnam
(where I've never been
though once ate
in a Vietnamese restaurant).

Sunset

Saint Peter's dome
going down
to yellow glow
of windows
across the lot and
yard and Great Wall of China
hedge,
like some muscled arm
that curls the road,
and over the cloud-tree
grove
a steel sphincter or splinter
or splint—whatever—
aimed across the brow
of twilight's far & near vistas
of Andean peaks and
rolling hills,
blue aquarium of
fishes
swimming in
bottled joy.

Friends

My best friends are Doug and Carrie
Heffernan from "The King of Queens."

I dreamt Doug ran in the Kentucky Derby
without a horse,
and won.

(How sad is that—best friends are TV sitcom
characters?

      1.   Very.
      2.   Quite.
      3.   Extremely.)

I dreamt I had sex with Carrie
and woke, pregnant.

I can't wait to see what
comes out, and
where—
if a boy I will name him
Pyrite.
If a girl
Myst.

Catholic

In school they called me 'Wally'
because I looked like Wally Cleaver.
The black kids asked me:
"Wally, have you seen Beaver?"
I gave them the finger, and
they chased me;
I ran like a gazelle around the
schoolyard each recess period…
I tried out for altar-boy
but got cut from the team
by an acne-scared priest who
smelled like
cloak—
I chose 'Daniel' as my
confirmation name:
he who, in the Bible, lived in the
lion's den.

Play

A fly with long pincer arms
and a fur coat on
says "so long" as
it exits
stage left, and
the clowns come on
as the hero, backstage
dies in the arms of the heroine
heir to fortune's favors
in *Mourning Becomes Electric.*

Gabble Goop

Goofy Gobbler from
downstairs—
on her porch,
perched:
gobble-gobble
gabba-
gobba,
popple
gapple
cackle-
cluckle.

Advise

You will be alright, Kid
hang in there
keep the chin up
something will turn up,
don't get your shorts in a knot—
go run a few laps,
say some prayers
ask god to help you
he just might
okay Kid?
And keep your pecker up
ha ha
don't turn down anything
that shows up
don't take any wooden nickels
either
and don't worry
things will turn out
you'll see!
And
hey!
Don't forget what I've said.

Honey,

I am leaving for Mars
Thursday.
Will take 8 months to
arrive: will call you on
arrival. The call
will take 2-3 weeks
to reach you.
PLEASE pick up.
Will return near the first
of the following year.
See you then?

Death

Is like being lost in the
woods
walking around trying
to get back to some place
recognizable, while
fighting the anxiety of
separation, until
finally
accepting your new indeterminate
condition, between
life, and living
death, and dying—
and then feeling anxiety free
as you begin to enjoy
being dead—
like a new career forced upon you;
one you fought against, but, once
started
found you like it; are
glad you made the change.

A fat man in a car
parked at the edge of the
park: He stares at me,
to glean the low-down,
the dope,
the skinny…
He is C.I.A., MOSSAD, KGB.
He reports to mission control
by speaking into the
glove compartment.

Vacay

She went on vacation
and when she returned
discovered her house gone
and no one could tell her
where—
a big truck, the authorities said
came and took it.
She moved into an apartment
and never did come to know
where her house went, but
one thing she knew for sure:
she would never go on vacation
again.

Sinners

Two guys hauling a tarp
full of leaves
from the lawn of the
church; a guy
at each end,
the tarp sagging
as if a body
within—
a church body who
died for sins
committed—
the lawn is swept clean
of him,
of whomever:
me, you, some commandment-
breaking bastard, or
the guy who
wrote 'em.

Sitting on a park bench
in the sun shine
as I write
this poem or
scribble
while a guy
who wants to borrow money
from me
stands nearby on a street corner
beneath circling pigeons...
A siren whines in the
distance
in this instance
of
life never ending.

Pick up the words again—
like a suitcase from the
terminal, and
add, subtract, revise—
no one ever wrote anything
good straight-out, or
I never have anyway;
maybe Shakespeare did
maybe Kerouac
but not me—
I am no Bard
Beat Daddio
or Bawd
either.
Lawd, no.

Storm

The darkness thickens
like a plot
and the river eddies, waiting
as
lights of the laundry
flicker, and
thunder follows
a scraggly scribbled bolt
of lightning that sets off
an alarm:
signal to cover or
cower, as
the Luftwaffe crosses the channel
and rain drops rap
like knuckles
on car roof tops.

Feeling alone and
lonely, can't make a connection—
it hurts
the pain upsets me,
I get pissed:
look around for someone
to blame
and decide on the waitress,
for not being friendlier, not
giving me a hug, or
a kiss…
I take a dollar off
her tip; to teach
her…What?
I stand on the roadside
staring at cars
speeding past, fleeing
from me.

Friend

A Kentucky license plate
Beneath a bumper sticker
FRIEND OF GOD
got some gall I think
as god cannot say
"no friend of mine,"
or maybe god can
but who would hear?
Kind of like a sticker
FRIEND OF COPS
Or
NO REAL FRIENDS, JUST GOD
JUST COPS.

Cold Snow World

Gray 6 a.m.
my car an igloo
in the lot—
Eskimo-dreams woke me
5:30 a. m.
not even a mouse
stirring and
rooftops of white dawn
which was my Indian name
when I lived with the
Facqwee tribe and
tee-peed the landscape
at five foot five
in my tadpole outfit
in the era
of the Giant Sloth
and Smilodon
stuck in tar pits
of
my mind.

A Nice Winter Day of

warm sun and
sparkling snow crust;
moon like a thumb print
in blue sky, and
crows drifting by, wings
flapping—
I sit on a park bench
that holds me upright
or prone
as the world whirls
through
time &
space.

Dream

The Woman's Major League Baseball
Homerun Champion—
She hit 55 during the
season, and
has big tits
besides—
I lie my head
on them
as the train, clickity-clack
down the track, takes us to the
Grand Canyon.

The Scary War

Hand-to-hand combat
with bayonets
in the trenches;
mini balls to tear
your arms off;
and if gut-shot, you
died—
a rifle heavy as
a pickax, a suit of
wool
baked in the
Southern sun;
must have been fun
though, riding on the
train roof, camping
beneath stars; taking
whatever you needed
when you wanted it—
ripping the guts out
the Secesch.

2.

2 men talking out of my
nose as I wake to morning's
gibberish

woke to acceptance
a smattering of
distant applause

idly spending the
last golden days of
autumn

Nietzsche

Nietzsche's sister and mother hid
him away on the second floor
behind his mustache and
the vines of a veranda
he walked
spouting gibberish
until the day he became silent—
the "Argonaut of the Spirit" had no more
to say, or else unable to
and nothing left to do
either
except ascend to
Vahalla where there are no anti-Semites
like his sister, and
no Germans either, like the Wagners
only Europeans, like
himself, souls
in sync, and
human, all too human.

Not Forgive

but
forget,
as Nietzsche said—
the capacity of an
aristocrat of
the mind, true
Dionysian,
letting go resentments
and hurts;
a conscious act
of forgetting
the bastards
the bitches
and then moving-on
with one's
so-called
life.

Under the Volcano

The luminous wheel turns: Ferris wheel,
Zodiac, infernal machine, in contrapuntal
delirium tremens style, symbolism strewn
like billboards along the roadside—and
how about that taxing Taxcala chapter?
How about Yvonne, fluttering like a butterfly
about the plot, and Hugh the fatuous brother-in-law
and "man of ideas," who survives, while el Senor Consul
dies, borracho, face down in Mehico, a victim or
volunteer, who knows? He goes into the barranca like
a pariah dog—like the world—1939—on this great day--
this Day of the Dead: not a Bloom's Day, but close.

Big Man

I am at the Academy Awards ceremony.
"Charles Bukowski" is called and
the great man appears on stage, riding
a bicycle, and I laugh (because
what a card!). On the big screen behind the
stage flashes a glossy movie-glam photo of
Buk: I call "Henry!" as he exits with his
award…I am there as a Red Buttons impersonator
trying to mimic Red Buttons' mannerisms when
speaking to
whomever, and wondering, as I do
if those I speak to 'get it'?
Do they know I am 'doing' Red Buttons?

3.

thanks a lot day

turkeys on the run
from hunters with
guns—
the mashed potatoes
balk
and being lumped with
the squash
and the cranberry sauce
laments the loss
of table space
to stuffing up
the orifice
of the state bird.

Stiff

I take walks in the
cemetery
where it is quiet;
none of the stiffs
makes a peep:
whatever they once had
fled at the
moment of death
and left them
fish-gray and
on a slab
until the mortician
stuffed each
like a Thanksgiving turkey
and painted the
faces, and
then they laid
in a box
for a day or two
until the start of
their bone-life
in the cemetery, skulls,
ribs, and such
not much to it
else, surely
we would have heard something
from them
by now.

I Am

unattached and
free-floating;
unaffiliated
and too small
to be picked-up
by radar
too stolid
to be
illusion,
too big to
be
microorganism,
too dense
to be wind
or light:
I am coming-in
under the wire
as "Kid Long-Shot."

Dying

is not that big a deal
unless you are the
one in the
box:
"poor —
gone so soon!
Looked good to me
last Saturday,
like not a care
in the world!"
The first shovelful of
dirt hits the coffin lid,
phat!
And you know
you are not getting back up
out of there;
not this time, no
not any time,
ever—
no one will dig you up,
you know that
splat!
Never be topside
again—
have to turn your back
on succulent Spring, beautiful
autumn, and
go
elsewhere.

Hidden

I lifted weights in the
cellar as
the furnace rumbled
on and off
and ghosts hung back in the
shadows
where Gramp had hidden the
booze
during Prohibition
when gangsters had knocked
at the back door:
Mugs and Bugs and Legs—
the bar room supported the
family, brothers, nephews, cousins;
Grandma and all her kin—
I return there in dreams
only the bar is a ship
landlocked, prow pointed
to the playground next door
of empty swings, bleachers, and
a merry-go-round.

4.

mailman drops new bill
"kerchunk" into
my box

gray puff-ball heads of
dandelions like elderly
blacks survived whitey
and gun shots

drooping heads of sunflowers
bowing
to the inevitable

Attack

Having shortness of breath and chest pain,
I thought "heart attack,' but
no
only arterial heart disease,
same as killed my father
at 33
high blood pressure and
stroke, he
collapsed in a grand mal
seizure
as I played on the stairs
with my Army men…
I remember his red & white checkered
bathrobe and
Gramp, standing, silhouette in the bathroom window
and
a man wearing
shiny shoes, and
carrying a black bag,
stepping over my soldiers
who looked up to me
awaiting the order
to attack the hillside.

Out Back

Knowing who in the neighborhood
to avoid
was key;
staying out of the grasp
of beefy moles wearing misshapen
hats and
with hairy paws
reaching to massage
shoulder or back
and who
given the chance
would drag you down
into the cellar and
dismember you part by part—
those dirty drooling misfits
of the heart
who lived under cars
or in sheds out back,
who kept playing pocket pool
as they talked,
whose gimlet eyes opened
like cracks;
ogres on street corners
whose faces shone in
attic windows
when the moon glowed.

No Poetry

There was no poetry in those days
and all the riverbeds were dried-up
and the leaves fallen off the
trees;
the grass was burnt brown
and we used rocks & sticks
as toys to play with:
it rained at least part of
every day
and the dumb bastards among us
talked all the time
while the lips of the
wise were sewn shut—
how did I survive?
I didn't.
I carry the scars from
the lava that ran
down the mountainsides;
still have holes from
where they bored into me
with their stares—
never did I despair though—
but came close.

Paul Bearer

At the funeral home I stood
aside from the crowd, hoping I did not
look like too big a jackass to
anyone.
A guy I did not know
stepped up to me and
asked: "And you are?"
"Pallbearer," I said.

Afterward, everyone went to
my uncle's house and
started to get smashed
in honor or remembrance, or
whatever, of my grandmother
who had been a raging alcoholic.

"Hello Paul," the guy I did not know
said. "Hello," I said.

My cousin Wally stole a bottle
and he and I went to his room
and drank it, then had a wrestling
match and tore up the furniture.

My Uncle appeared in the doorway,
a look of disappointment spread over
his red beefy face. He said that it
was alright to have fun and
even to raise some hell but
there was a limit to it, and
a guy had to know his limits;
he said that my father and he
raised hell when they were
young too but knew when to
stop; knew their limits; he
said my father (who died young)
had been a tough son of a bitch
and that he was a tough son of a bitch
too and that Wally and I were tough
sons a bitches, and his arm dropped
off my shoulder and he went
downstairs for a refill as Wally and
I began tearing the rest of the room
up, and Grandma
lay in the cemetery, no longer
to neglect or abuse
anyone.

Acknowledgements

I would like to thank and acknowledge the following publications, in which many of these poems first appeared: Cajun Mutt Press, Dumpster Press, The Dope Fiend Daily, Terror House Magazine, Dissident News, Lothlorien Poetry Journal, A Thin Slice of Anxiety, 13 Myna Birds, Torrid Literature, Roadside Raven Review, Rust Belt Review, Unlikely Stories, Piker Press, Heroin Love Songs, Pangolin Review, Haikuniverse, Bear Creek Haiku, The Rye Whiskey Review, Under the Bleachers, Bardball, Five Fleas, Meat for Tea, and The Screech Owl.

Wayne F. Burke

www.ingramcontent.com/pod-product-compliance
Lightning Source LLC
Chambersburg PA
CBHW050225100526
44585CB00017BA/2011